Changes

Program Authors

Connie Juel, Ph.D.

Jeanne R. Paratore, Ed.D.

Deborah Simmons, Ph.D.

Sharon Vaughn, Ph.D.

Glenview, Illinois
Boston, Massachusetts
Chandler, Arizona
Hoboken, New Jersey

ISBN-13: 978-0-328-45271-2
ISBN-10:   0-328-45271-8

15   16

Changes

Growing and Changing

Changes in Nature

Contents

Places Change

See page 29 for My New Words and Pictionary!

Places Change

Pam has a little pet shop.
Pam sells fish at her shop.

Mom looks at fish as Josh naps.

Look at the pet shop now!
It got big but not that big.

Mom and Josh stop at the shop.
Josh asks Mom to get him a fish.

See the pet shop now!

Pam still sells fish.

But she sells crabs and frogs as well.

Will Mom let Josh get a pet frog?
Not just yet. Josh must grow a bit.

Look! Now the pet shop is Pet Land!
Pam sells lots of pets at her shop.

At last Josh is a big kid.
Josh can use cash to get a pet frog!

A City Snapshot

by Joy Lockwood • illustrated by Greg LaFever

Look at this land!
It is a grand spot for shops.
But it has just one shop.

Beth has her cloth shop at this spot.

Click! Click! Snap a shot!

Look at this land now!
It is still a spot for shops.
But now it has lots of shops.

Seth has a rug shop. Trish sells eggs.

Shel can use help in his hat shop.

Click! Click! Snap a shot!

Look! What is this land now?
Now it is a big, big city.

It has blocks and blocks of shops.
You must look up to see the tops!
Click! Click! Snap a shot!

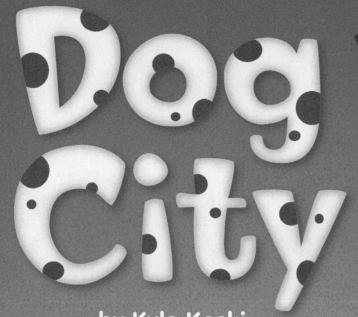

Dog City

by Kyle Koski

illustrated by
Christine Schneider

Tish looks at her pups.
Sh! Kip, Nip, and Pip nap.

Can they all fit on the red bed?
Yes. But the pups are still small.

Kip, Nip, and Pip grow big.
Beth pats them. "Go in, pups!"
The pups go in.

"Go in, Tish!" Beth calls.
But Tish can not go in.
They can not all fit!

Beth and Dad talk.
They have a plan.

Tap! Tap! Tap!
Tish and her pups look.
Can Beth and Dad help?

Look! Pip has a bed.
Kip has a bed.
And Nip has a bed!

All the pups have beds.
Now Tish can use her red bed.
Call it Dog City!

Which Way Is the Pet Shop?

School Street

Elm Street

Lake Street

Main Street

Dad, Beth, and Tish need to go to the pet shop. Use your finger to show how they can get there.

How can they get to the park?

My New Words

grow   A pup will **grow** up to be a dog.

her*   We have **her** book.
             Give **her** this book.

now*   Walk the dog **now.**

use*   We **use** an umbrella to stay dry.

*tested high-frequency words

Pictionary

city

land

Contents

Learning New Things

See page 53 for My New Words and Pictionary!

Learning New Things

Little kids can not do a lot.

Kids must get help.

Moms and dads must help them.

Kids get big.

But kids can make a mess.

Kids want moms and dads to help.

Kids get big.
Big kids can do a lot.
But moms and dads can still help.

Moms and dads want to make
all kids safe.

Now the same kids are old.
The same kids are moms and dads.

They can help kids too.

Kids Can Do Lots

by Kim Lee

Swish!

In grade 1, kids are not too old.

But kids can do lots.

What can you do?

In grade 1, kids like fun games.
Kids can make faces. Look at
that face! Can you make faces?

In grade 1, kids can skate.
Kids can skate from place to place.

Zoom!

Kids want to race and skate fast.
Can you skate?

In grade 1, kids can hit balls.
Kids can hit them past bases.
Can you hit balls?

In grade 1, kids can do lots.
What can you do?

Jake
and the
Surprise

by Daniel Ortiz
illustrated by Barry Gott

"Look at this page," said Mom.

Dad did.

"Jake is age six on that date," said
Mom. "We can get Jake gifts."

"Yes, but what will Jake want?"
said Dad.

Just then, Jake came in.

Mom had to spell the gifts that
she will get.
"P-e-t-s in a c-a-g-e," said Mom.

But Jake gave Mom and Dad a surprise too.

"Mom and Dad, I am in grade 1," said Jake. "I am old and big."

"Yes," said Mom and Dad.

"And I can s-p-e-l-l *pets* and *cage*," said Jake.

Dad had a big grin on his face.

"You are not too old for big, big
h-u-g-s," said Mom.

"Not yet," said Jake.

And that is just what Mom
gave him!

This Is the Way We Sing a Song

This is the way we brush our teeth,
Brush our teeth, brush our teeth.
This is the way we brush our teeth,
So early in the morning.

This is the way we brush our hair . . .
This is the way we read a book . . .
This is the way we sing a song . . .

What else do you do in the morning?

My New Words

old*   The **old** wall has a crack.
            Jake is six years **old**.

too*   She can run and jump **too**.
            She can not run **too** fast.

want*   The kids **want** a big snack.

*tested high-frequency words

Pictionary

gift

surprise

Contents

We All Grow

We All Grow

Look! There is a baby duck.

It was in this shell.
But now it is not.

Baby Duck is not this big yet.
Who is?
Its mom and dad are this size.

In time, Baby Duck will get just as big.

Look at this baby fish!
Where are your fins, Baby Fish?

It will get fins. It will get big.
Fins help big fish swim.

Look! Baby Trish can smile.
But Trish can not stand up yet.

Will Trish stand up one day? Yes!
Trish will get big like Mom.

Baby Duck

by Patricia Wydell

An egg jumps in a nest.
Tap! Tap!
Who is in there?

The thin white shell cracks.
It is a baby duck!

This new duck can not stand up yet.
Sh! Rest a while, Baby Duck.

Swish! Swish! Ducks swim in a line.
Is Baby Duck with them? Yes!
Kick your legs, Baby Duck!

Is it time for a snack?
Whap! Baby Duck snaps up a bug.

When will Baby Duck get big?
Just look! That day has come!

Big
and
Small

by Pete Hill

illustrated by
Luciana Navarro Powell

Mitch is big. Mitch is six.
Liz is small. Liz is still a baby.

Can Liz walk? Not too much.
Liz still falls a lot. But Mitch is
there to catch her.

Can Liz chat with Mitch?

Not too much. Liz can call Mitch.

Then Mitch smiles at Liz.

Can Liz stack the blocks?
Not too much. Her blocks fall.
Mitch helps Liz make a new pile.

Can Liz swim? Not yet.
Liz is just a tot.

Who can swim then? Mitch can.
Mitch swims like a champ!

Will Liz get big? Yes!
We all grow up.

Your time will come, Liz.
You will get big like Mitch.

SECRET

Read Together

by Beverly McLoughland

Mrs. Kangaroo,
Is it true,
Are you hiding
Someone new
In the pocket
Part of you?
There must be someone
New and growing,
His little ears
Have started showing.

My New Words

day   A week lasts 7 **days**. Each **day** is made up of 24 hours.

there*   Is **there** a park near here?

who*   **Who** is at the door?

your*   **Your** blocks are under the chair.

*tested high-frequency words

Pictionary

new

$2.00

baby

Contents

How Does a Garden Change?

See page 107 for My New Words and Pictionary!

How Does a Garden Change?

winter

The pond froze.
This garden was just a big
patch of ice.

Plants could not poke up in the ice, not yet.

spring

Then ice gets thin and melts.
Wet drops fall and fall on
the garden.

Grass gets very green and tall.
Buds pop up on stems of garden
plants.

summer

Next the sun is hot.
Gardens fill with red and
yellow roses.

Can your nose smell these roses?

Mine can.

Bugs buzz and eat bits of plants.

fall

Then winds chill gardens.
Winds nip your nose.

Plants get set to rest.
Ice will be back.

BUGS!

by Lin Chen

Stop and look at gardens.
You'll spot bugs, lots and lots of them.

Bugs buzz past your nose!
Bugs walk on plants and stones.

Green Stink Bug

But you can't spot all bugs.
Small bugs can hide very well.

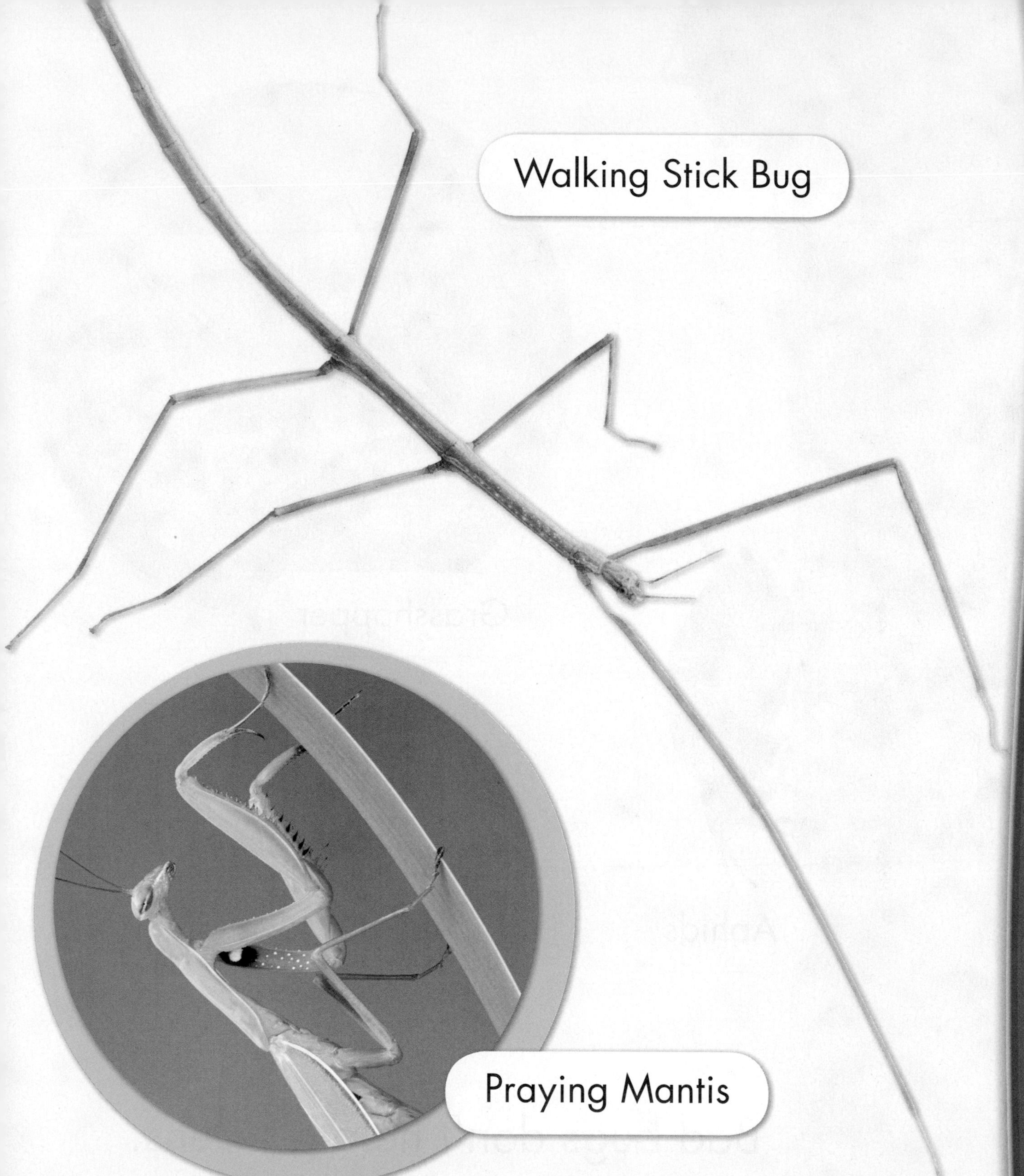

Walking Stick Bug

Praying Mantis

And bugs can look like stems and sticks.

Grasshopper

Aphids

Bad bugs don't help gardens.
Bad bugs eat stems and
buds and vines.

Japanese Beetle

Bad bugs could eat too much!
Bad bugs can kill plants.

Ladybug

But bugs can help gardens too.
They'll eat bad plants and bad bugs.

Butterfly

Bumblebee

Bugs can help plants get big.
All gardens can use bugs that help!

Worms Help Plants

by Sonia Muñoz
illustrated by Jason Wolff

Yikes, Kid! Do not step on this white stone! You could step on me. And if you step on me, it'll make plants very sad!

Yes, I'm just a small worm!
But worms help make nice dirt.
Plants like that. And plants like us.

Dirt is the place I call home.
I do not like it when that home is wet.

If it is wet, I rest on stones and rocks.
If dirt isn't wet, I slide back in it.

Plant bits fall in dirt.
I will munch and munch on them.
And I will eat bits of bugs!

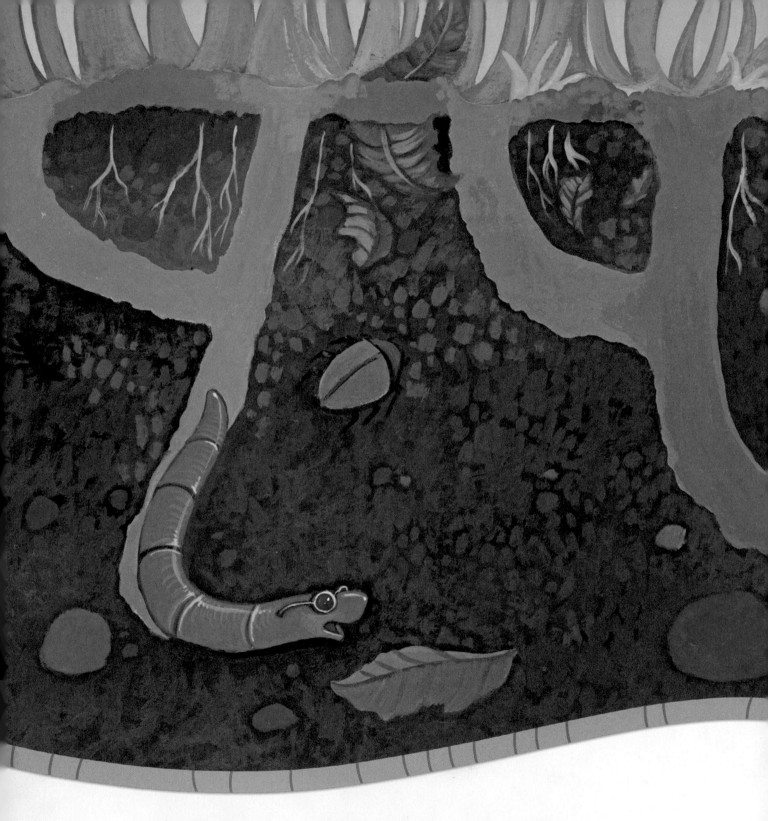

While I munch, I dig small
holes in the dirt.
I dig lots and lots of small holes.

Those small holes make nice dirt!
And all those holes help plants.

You can see that plants like me.
Worms can make nice dirt.
That helps plants get big and tall.

Now, Kid, help save this worm!
Step on that stone and not on this one!

Plant Parts

flower

leaf

leaf

stem

stem

root

roots

Name the parts
of the plants.
Which can you eat?

My New Words

could*   She **could** jump well.

eat*   When you **eat**, you chew and swallow food.

very*   July was **very** hot this year.

*tested high-frequency words

Pictionary

 dirt

garden

worm

Contents

Watch What Changes

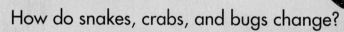

See page 129 for My New Words and Pictionary!

109

Watch What Changes

A small white egg rests on a plant.
When will this small white egg hatch?
And what will pop out?

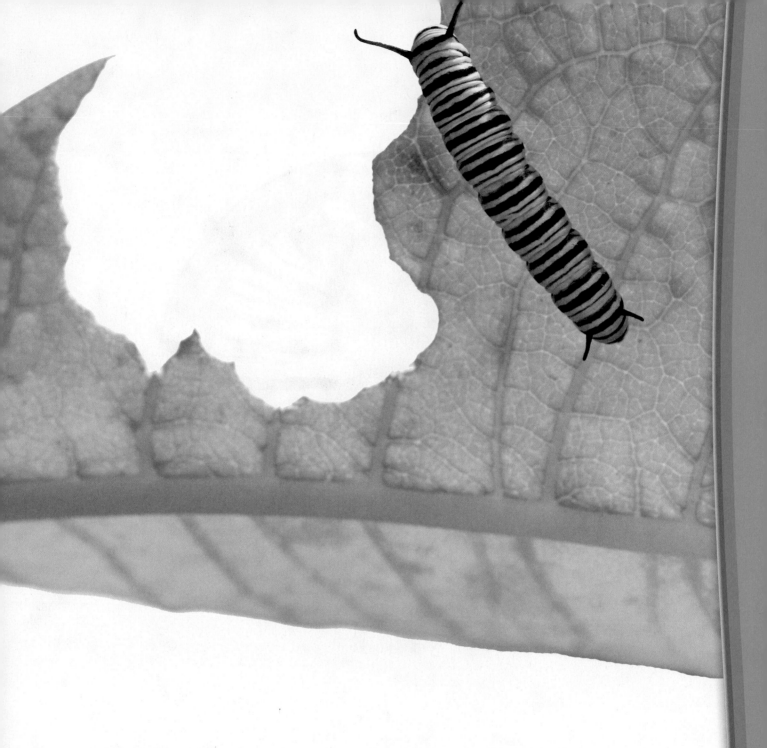

That white egg we saw did hatch.
This small caterpillar came out.
This small caterpillar eats lots and lots.

Take a good look at this caterpillar.
It makes its shell on this twig.

What is next?
What will it use this shell for?

At last, it sheds its shell.

What is it?
It is a nice big butterfly.
It is a huge butterfly!

The Same

by Alison Laine

Can we see snakes change?
This snake has shed its old skin.

It gets fresh skin.
But it is still the same snake.

Can we see this crab change?
Crabs need good shells.
They can use shells left out on the sand.

This crab seems like the same
crab we just saw.
It is. This is the same crab with a
good shell!

This bug changes a lot.
It is small.
Then it gets big.

See it on the tree? It is big and green.

Snakes, crabs, and bugs can change.
But they are still the same.

What Am I?

by Lee Tsang

illustrated by Don Tate

Out on a tree branch sits Fuzz.

Fuzz seems just like a cute worm.

But she keeps asking, "What am I?"

This is Tad.

Tad swims in Green Pond.

Tad swims just like a good fish.

But he keeps asking, "What am I?"

Fuzz sees Tad in Green Pond.

"Am I a worm?" Fuzz asks.

"Yes!" yells Tad. "Am I a fish?"

"Yes!" yells Fuzz.

Then Fuzz hides in an odd shell.
She can't see Tad.

Tad can't spot the worm he saw.

Next, Tad feels big changes.

He has legs! He has feet! He can walk!

Then Fuzz gets free from her shell.
"I am a butterfly," she yells and smiles.

And Tad hops from pad to pad.
"I am a frog," he yells and smiles.

A Frog's Life

A frog starts as an egg.

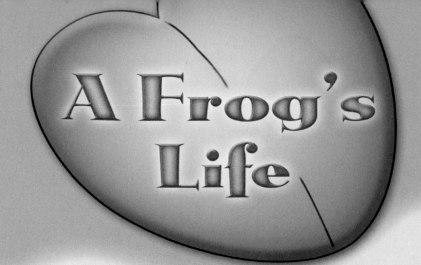

A tadpole hatches.

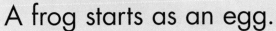

Back legs grow.

Look! It's a frog!

Front legs grow.

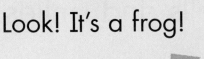

128

My New Words

good*   A **good** person or animal is kind and behaves well.

out*   We went **out** the door. The lights went **out**.

saw*   She **saw** a bird yesterday.

*tested high-frequency words

Pictionary

butterfly

caterpillar

Contents

When Seasons Change

When Seasons
Change

Hot, hot weeks are here!
Yellow sun shines down.

Tall trees are dressed in green.
Bees seem to buzz with life and fun.

Hot weeks have passed.
Trees are dressed in red and yellow.

Plants and bugs feel a big chill
on the way.

Winter hides sleeping plants and grass.
Ice bends tall trees.

Ponds freeze and kids skate.
This chill will not last.

The ice has melted now.
Hot sun is back at work.

Green buds have filled the trees.
Chicks peep and plants get tall.

Winter Changes

by David Elliot

Will this rabbit look the same all the time?
Last winter this rabbit was white.
That helped it hide.

Now it is not white.
Can it still hide?

Lakes freeze in winter.
Ducks go to a hot place.

But ducks come back when winter has passed.

This animal will take a big nap.
It will sleep all winter.

It is hidden deep down in this cave.
What will happen if we wake it up?

This small animal can't get nuts in winter.
It must work and save nuts now.

This way it can still munch on nuts all winter.

What Time Is Best?

by Maria Polomarkaki   illustrated by Maribel Suarez

What time is best? Is it summer?

Is it fall? Is it winter?

Is it spring? Let me see.

Last summer, we ran in the sand.

We dashed with kites. Zip!

We hid. Hide and seek! Peek!

I like summer.

Last fall, Dennis passed me the ball.
I passed it back in a flash.

We had on thick plastic helmets.
We crashed. Crack!
We ran fast and had fun. I like fall.

Last winter, Ellen and I rode sleds.

We walked up big hills.

Thump! Thump! That felt like work!

We yelled and dashed down
those big hills. I like winter.

Last spring, Dad and Mom walked with me way up on Blossom Hill.
We had a lunch basket. Keep out, ants!
We had a nice picnic. I like spring.